# Come to Tea!

## Fun Tea Party Themes, Recipes, Crafts, Games, Etiquette and More

**Stephanie Dunnewind**

**illustrated by Capucine Mazille**

Sterling Publishing Co., Inc.
New York

*To Zack and Zoë — S.D.*
*To Chloe — C.M.*

Edited by Isabel Stein
Book design by Spinning Egg Design Group, Inc.

**Library of Congress Cataloging-in Publication Data**

Dunnewind, Stephanie

  Come to tea; fun tea party themes, recipes, crafts, games, etiquette, and more/
Stephanie Dunnewind; illustrated by Capuchine Mazille.
    p. cm.
  Summary: Provides instructions for creating several different tea parties, with such
themes as a princess party, a teddy bears' picnic, and a pajama breakfast tea party.
Includes recipes, games, crafts and other activities.
  ISBN 0-8069-7899-6
    1. Afternoon teas—Juvenile literature. 2. Children's parties—Juvenile literature. [1.
Afternoon teas. 2. Parties. 3. Cookery.] I. Mazille, Capuchine, ill. II. Title.

TX736 .D85 2002
641.5'3—dc21                                                              2002021837

10  9  8  7  6  5  4  3  2  1

Published by Sterling Publishing Co., Inc.
387 Park Avenue South, New York, N.Y. 10016
© 2002 by Stephanie Dunnewind
Distributed in Canada by Sterling Publishing
C/o Canadian Manda Group, One Atlantic Avenue, Suite 105
Toronto, Ontario, Canada M6K 3E7
Distributed in Great Britain and Europe by Chris Lloyd at Orca Book Services,
Stanley House, Fleets Lane, Poole BH15 3AJ, England
Distributed in Australia by Capricorn Link (Australia) Pty. Ltd.
P.O. Box  704, Windsor, NSW 2756 Australia
*Printed in China*
*All rights reserved*

Sterling  ISBN 0-8069-7899-6

# Contents

· · · · · · · · · · · · · ·

# Introduction

This book will help you host your own tea party, offering ideas for food, games, crafts, and other activities. The basic idea of a tea party — drinking from delicate cups, serving dainty finger foods, dressing up, and using one's best manners — is a good one, even if you don't drink real tea.

The theme parties in this book could work for birthdays or special occasions with a large group of girls, a small circle of friends, or you and a special friend or relative. Don't feel obligated to host a party exactly as it is written. Choose recipes, games, and crafts from several parties to fit what you like and what you think your guests will enjoy. To make it easier to find what you want, check the index at the back of the book.

Even if you decide to make another party, read through the first party, the Classic Tea Party, as it gives helpful tips and general information.

Before making any food or crafts or using good china or tablecloths, check with a parent to make sure your plan is acceptable and to ask for help. Read through a recipe before you start making it, and assemble your tools and materials. You may need an adult to shop for supplies, turn on the oven or microwave, handle hot things, pour boiling water, cut up food, etc.

Invite a friend to help you prepare for your party — getting ready for a party is sometimes as much fun as actually having it! Most important of all, enjoy your guests and your party.

# A Note to Parents

Tea parties are favorites with young girls because they get a chance to play grownups with their friends, dressing up and using special dishes. Adult guests get down at a child's level, eating on doll-size dishes and sitting at a small table. For a little while, anyway, everyone gets along and minds their manners, civilized and entertained by the simple beverage and its accompaniments. While girls think it's all fun, you know they are learning skills that will serve them all their lives, such as cooking, using proper etiquette, and socializing.

We suggest you read through each party and decide which recipes and activities are most appropriate for your child and her friends and how much assistance and supervision in the kitchen are necessary. We hope you will find preparing for a tea party a fun way to spend time with your daughter.

# Tea Manners

* Don't start serving until everyone is seated.

* At a formal tea, the hostess pours the tea for everyone. At an informal gathering, set out a couple of teapots and let guests help themselves.

* When you are done stirring, place your teaspoon on the saucer.

* Put your napkin on your lap. Blot or pat your lips, rather than wiping your napkin across your mouth. Don't drink if your mouth has food in it.

* Remember to say "please" and "thank you" when asking others to pass you dishes. At the table, pass dishes to your right.

* Sit up straight and don't tip the chair.

# Hostess Tips

* Send out invitations two weeks in advance.

* RSVP stands for "please reply" in French. If you put RSVP on your invitation, polite guests should tell you in advance whether they are coming. This allows you to plan your menu, place settings, and party favors (but it never hurts to have a few extras on hand just in case).

* Keep the party size manageable but try not to leave out friends from a particular group who are likely to talk to each other.

6

* Write thank-you notes to all attendees, especially if they brought gifts.

* When guests RSVP, ask about any food allergies so you can plan your menu accordingly.

* Bookmark the pages of this book that you are going to use or write down the games and rules on a piece of paper or index card before the party.

* Plan a simple activity to keep early guests busy until everyone arrives.

* Before the party, make samples of all art projects you plan to use. This way you know that you have all materials on hand and have an example to show guests. Have extra materials on hand.

* Stay flexible. If a game doesn't go over well, skip quickly to the next one. Have more ideas than you think you'll use — just in case.

* If you have last-minute dishes to make, ask for a parent's help so you can spend your time with your guests instead of being in the kitchen, but do as much food preparation as possible before the party.

# Classic Tea Party

**W**ith classic tea sandwiches, a teapot-topped cake, and teacup crafts, this party is about everything tea! Even if you plan to choose one of the other theme parties, read this one, as it serves as a good base for all the others. You'll find directions for making invitations, decorations, crafts, games, and food. There are also tips for making a great cup of tea and tea sandwiches.

# Invitations

Fold a piece of paper in fourths to make a card. Draw or copy an outline of a teapot onto a thin piece of cardboard for a pattern. Cut out the pattern shape and trace it on the front of the card. Decorate the cards with marking pens, stickers, and glitter and write the invitation information inside.

**What to include on an invitation:**

- Party theme (be clear whether the tea party also is a birthday party so guests know to bring gifts)
- Hostess's name
- Date and time of party
- Location, including address, and directions if necessary
- Your phone number
- RSVP
- Special requests such as "Come dressed up" or "Bring a teddy bear." The basic information above is the same for all the parties.

# Decorations

## Outdoors

Trace or draw a teapot shape on cardboard to make a yard sign. Write WELCOME TO [YOUR NAME'S] TEA PARTY on the sign and decorate it. Draw teapots on a bunch of colored helium balloons if you wish.

## Indoors

Use a pretty cloth tablecloth with a lace runner down the center or paper doilies, set with pretty cups and plates. (Instead of cloth, you could buy solid-colored paper napkins and a paper tablecloth and decorate them with rubber ink stamps to match the party's theme.) Make a centerpiece of fresh flowers in a teapot or sugar bowl. Set your refreshments out on platters or plates covered with paper doilies.

# Place Cards

Cut a 2 × 3 inch (5 × 7.5 cm) piece of heavy construction paper or card stock. Fold in half lengthwise. Write a guest's name on the front; then trace with a thin line of glue. Break open a bag of black tea and sprinkle tea leaves so they completely cover the glue. Gently shake off any excess; let the glue dry. Make one for each guest. Set the card next to the girl's plate.

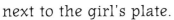

# Refreshments

- Grandma's Sweet Tea

- Simple Cucumber Sandwiches

- Teapot-Topped Cake

## How to Make and Serve a Great Cup of Tea

* Reminder: Have an adult help you prepare and serve all hot drinks. Fill a teakettle with cold water and heat to a boil. Remove as soon as it starts to boil. Boiling it too long makes the water lose oxygen, and then the tea will taste flat.

* After the water heats, warm the teapot by pouring in some hot water and pouring it out.

* If you have loose tea, measure a teaspoonful (5 mL) for each cup plus one extra "for the pot." With tea bags, use one less than the number of cups of water in the teapot. Allow to steep 3 to 5 minutes.

* When removing tea bags, let them drip into the pot but don't squeeze, as pressing the brewed leaves can leave a bitter flavor. If you use loose tea, pour through a strainer into cups.

* Black tea has less than half as much caffeine as coffee, but it still has some. All the recipes in this book call for decaffeinated tea or herbal teas that are naturally caffeine-free.

* Let tea cool before serving to children so there is no risk of burned tongues or fingers.

* With black teas, offer milk, but not cream, which is too rich for tea. If you are worried that the tea is too hot, serve the milk cold; otherwise, serve it at room temperature so it won't cool the tea too much. Adding milk should be optional as some people don't like milk in tea.

* Use pretty dishes to put out lemon slices and sugar or honey to flavor tea. Note: Lemon can cause milk to curdle, so don't use both together.

## Grandma's Sweet Tea

Makes about 20 cups of tea

**Ingredients:**
- 2 cups (480 mL) powdered orange drink
- ½ cup (120 mL) decaffeinated instant tea
- 1 small packet (3.6 g) of powdered sweetened lemonade
- 1 teaspoon (5 mL) cinnamon
- ½ teaspoon (2.5 mL) cloves
- 1 cup (240 mL) sugar

1. Mix all ingredients in a medium bowl. Store in an airtight container until ready to use.

2. Spoon 2 tablespoons (30 mL) of the mixture into a cup, pour in hot water, and stir. Or add 2 tablespoons (30 mL) per cup of water to a teapot.

# Simple Cucumber Sandwiches

Makes 4 small sandwiches

**Ingredients:**

- Cucumber
- 1 oz (28 g) butter or cream cheese
- 2 pieces of thin-sliced white bread

1. Use a vegetable peeler to peel a cucumber. Ask a parent to thinly slice the cucumber into rounds.

2. Lightly spread butter or cream cheese on two slices of thin-sliced white bread. Arrange cucumber slices on one slice of bread; top with the second. Ask a parent to help you cut off the crusts.

3. Cut the sandwich in quarters or use a cookie cutter to make shaped sandwiches.

# More Creative Sandwiches

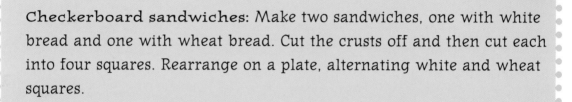

**Open-faced sandwiches:** Use a cookie cutter to make shapes out of bread. Cut the same shapes out of meat or cheese. Top the bread shapes with cheese or meat shapes and decorate with mustard and pieces of carrots, tomatoes, cucumbers, and nuts, black olives, grapes, or pickles.

**Checkerboard sandwiches:** Make two sandwiches, one with white bread and one with wheat bread. Cut the crusts off and then cut each into four squares. Rearrange on a plate, alternating white and wheat squares.

**Biscuit sandwiches:** Cut biscuit dough into shapes with cookie cutters. Bake on a cookie sheet. After baking, slice biscuits in half and use for sandwiches.

## Tea Sandwich Tips

* Thinly spread both slices of bread with butter, peanut butter, or cream cheese. This keeps the sandwich from getting soggy.

* Let butter and cream cheese soften at room temperature for an hour or so before you spread them so they don't rip the bread.

* Buy special thin-sliced bread at the grocery store. If you use regular bread, slightly flatten each slice with a rolling pin before using.

# Teapot-Topped Cake

See package for portions

**Ingredients:**

- Package of cake mix and any extra ingredients called for on the package.*
- Set of doll teacups and teapot or tea party candle cake decorations

*Or use your own favorite cake recipe.

1. Prepare and bake a packaged cake mix or your favorite cake according to the directions. Let cake cool and remove from pan.

2. Ice the cake (see icing recipe). Top the cake with a set of doll teacups and teapot or tea party candles.

# Butter Frosting (Icing)

For one cake.

**Ingredients:**

- ⅓ cup (80 mL) margarine, softened
- 2 to 3 tablespoons (30 to 45 mL) milk
- 4 cups (960 mL) confectioner's sugar
- 1 teaspoon (5 mL) vanilla

1. In a bowl, cream the margarine (beat until it's soft).

2. Add the remaining ingredients, starting with 2 tablespoons (30 mL) milk, and beat until smooth. Add additional milk as needed to thin the frosting.

# Crafts

## DECORATING TEACUPS

You Will Need:

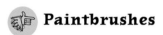 **Inexpensive plastic or ceramic teacups**

**Acrylic paints, including clear gloss finish**

**Paintbrushes**

**1.** Give each guest a cup to paint at the beginning of the party so the cups have time to dry. It might take a half-hour or more. Keep paint away from the rims of the cups.

**2.** When dry, coat with a clear enamel gloss acrylic paint to keep the design from scratching off.

# Games and Other Activities

## TEA PLATTER MEMORY GAME

Arrange teacups, teapot, and other objects on a tea platter. Have girls observe for one minute, then close eyes. Remove or change one thing. The first one to notice the change wins.

## TEAPOT

One player, It, leaves the room. The rest decide on a word. When It comes back, girls take turns saying sentences, substituting the word "teapot" for the chosen word. It must guess the word. Whoever gave the sentence is then It.

16

## Afternoon Tea

* Anna, Duchess of Bedford, popularized the afternoon tea in England in the mid 1800s. Anna got hungry between lunch and dinner; dinner sometimes wasn't served until 8 or 9 p.m. She asked for tea, cakes, and sandwiches to nibble on during the afternoon, and soon other Victorian women were following suit.

* Tea is served between 3 and 6 p.m. Typically, the earlier the hour, the lighter the food. Afternoon tea is usually served on a tray or cart, rather than at a table.

* Three types of food are traditionally served: first, comfort foods such as muffins, scones, biscuits, and toast; then small sandwiches; then sweets.

* As a general rule, serve scones and sandwiches with the first cup of tea and sweets with the second.

* Traditionally, teas feature all finger food so people can eat and hold their teacups.

* "High tea" is actually more of a dinner, with hearty meat dishes.

## Party Favors

Stuff candy and tea bags in a party bag. Add each girl's decorated teacup when dry to the favor bag and tie with a ribbon.

# Princess Tea Party

**T**ea and royalty have always gone together. When first introduced in England, tea had a very high price, which made it a drink of the upper class only. Princess Catherine of Braganza (Portugal) brought a large chest of tea as part of her dowry when she married Charles II of England. With the cultivation of tea in India, the price got lower. Queen Victoria encouraged the custom of taking afternoon tea, and many teapots were inscribed "God Bless Our Queen." You can invite fellow princesses to join you at your castle for a tea party befitting royal highnesses.

# Invitations

Draw a castle shape on thin cardboard for a pattern. Cut it out. Draw a door shape on another piece of cardboard, and cut it out as a pattern. For each invitation, trace the castle on a piece of construction paper. Trace the door on another piece of construction paper and cut it out. On the front of the door, write YOU'RE INVITED. Attach the top of the door paper to the castle paper with a bit of glue or tape. Write the party information on the castle underneath the door.

# Decorations

## Outside

Put up posterboard arrow signs in the yard saying THIS WAY TO PRINCESS [YOUR NAME]'S CASTLE or make arrows with chalk on the sidewalk. Hang cloth or kraft paper banners on either side of the front door. Draw or paint a decoration (a castle or dragon, for example) on each banner, if you wish.

# Inside

Princesses live in high style, so ask Mom if you can use your nice dishes and a pretty tablecloth. If you have a play crown or tiara, set it around a low dish and fill the dish with flowers for a centerpiece. Decorate each chair with streamers or garlands so it looks like a throne.

## CARDBOARD CASTLE CENTERPIECE

You Will Need:

**Four cardboard rolls from toilet paper**

**Strong glue and tape**

**Acrylic or tempera paint**

**Construction paper**

**Craft sticks and scissors**

1. Using scissors, cut rectangular pieces out of one end of each of four cardboard rolls, leaving parts sticking up between them, so they look like castle turrets (little towers).

2. Stand all four tubes on their uncut ends and glue the tubes' sides together (see illustration). It's easiest to glue two tubes together with a stripe of glue down the side and then add the third and fourth.

3. Paint the whole thing gray or whatever color you like. Cut windows and a door from black construction paper and glue to the castle.

4. Make a drawbridge by taping or gluing together four craft sticks with a few across underneath for strength. Attach it to the front of the castle. Decorate a tower with a paper flag.

# Place Cards

For each card, cut a 2 × 5 inch (5 × 7.5 cm) rectangle of heavy construction paper or card stock. Fold in half lengthwise. On the front write PRINCESS [GUEST'S NAME] with a pencil and then trace it with glue. Put the card over a newspaper, sprinkle glitter over the glue, and shake the card to remove any excess.

# Refreshments

- Strawberry Tea Punch
- Jewel Tea Biscuits
- Truffles

## Strawberry Tea Punch

Makes 16 half-cup servings

**Ingredients:**

- 8 cups (2 L) decaffeinated tea, cooled
- 12 oz (360 mL) frozen lemonade concentrate
- 16 oz (480 mL) frozen strawberries with sugar

1. Stir the lemonade and strawberries into the cooled tea.

2. Chill and serve.

# Jewel Tea Biscuits

See biscuit mix box for servings

**Ingredients:**

- Box of biscuit mix and whatever other ingredients are listed on the box
- A little flour
- Cooking oil spray
- Jam or jelly

1. Have a parent heat the oven as directed on the package. Make a batch of biscuit dough.

2. With a rolling pin, roll the dough out on a clean, lightly floured surface to about one-quarter inch (6 mm) thick. With a large biscuit cutter (or a round glass), cut circles in the dough. Place half the circles on a lightly oiled cookie sheet, about an inch (2.5 cm) apart.

3. With a smaller cutter (or a shot glass), cut a hole in the middle of each of the remaining circles to make rings.

4. Place the rings on top of the whole circles. Put a teaspoonful of jam or jelly in the middle of each ring.

5. Set the small center circles you cut out on another oiled cookie sheet. These will bake more quickly than the larger biscuits, so take them out earlier if you bake the cookie sheets together. Ask a parent to help you bake the biscuits about 12 to 15 minutes, or until golden.

6. Ask a parent to remove the biscuits from the oven and immediately lift them onto a plate or towel-lined basket. Serve warm.

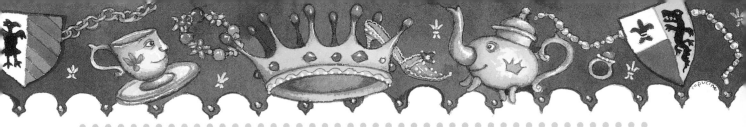

# Truffles

Makes 6 truffles

**Ingredients:**

- 1 cup (240 mL) chocolate chips
- ¼ cup (60 mL) butter cut into small pieces
- ½ teaspoon (2.5 mL) vanilla extract
- 5 tablespoons (75 mL) unsweetened cocoa
- 5 tablespoons (75 mL) powdered sugar

1. Mix chocolate chips, butter, and vanilla in microwave-proof bowl. Have a parent microwave on high 1 minute, stir, and then microwave another minute until melted. Stir with wooden spoon until smooth. Refrigerate one hour.

2. Mix cocoa and sugar together on a large plate. Using a teaspoon and your hands, make half-inch (12 mm) balls of the cold chocolate mixture. Roll balls in the cocoa mixture. Store in your refrigerator in an airtight container.

# Crafts

### PRINCESS CROWNS

You Will Need:

**4 × 25 inch (10 × 64 cm) strips of kraft paper or thick wrapping paper, one for each guest***

**Stapler or tape**

**Markers, stickers, stars, and plastic jewels for decoration**

**Notepad or something with a corner**

**Scissors**

*If you don't want to make crowns, buy paper gold crowns at a craft store.

**1.** Use the corner of a notepad or something rectangular to trace points on one long edge of a paper strip. Cut away the paper between the points so there is a sawtooth edge on one long side. This paper will become a crown.

**2.** Let each girl decorate her crown with markers, stickers, etc.

**3.** Have a parent shape the decorated paper around the girl's head, overlapping the ends to fit her head. Remove from head and staple or tape the crown so it stays.

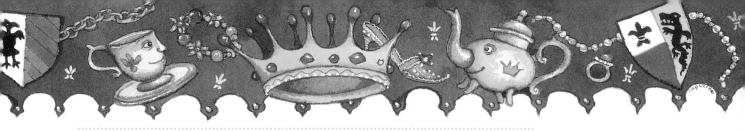

# Games and Other Activities

### PRINCESS CHARADES

Act out a fairy tale without speaking, using hand motions. Other girls have to guess which one. You can also divide into teams and see who guesses first. Some suggestions: The Princess and the Pea, Rapunzel, Snow White.

### CINDERELLA SHOE HUNT

Mix all the girls' shoes in a pile. One by one, blindfold the girls and make them find their own shoes and then put them on. Or divide them into teams and compete in a relay race without blindfolds. Each girl tags the next one after she finds her shoes; the first team in which all the girls are wearing their own shoes wins.

### PRINCESS DRESS-UP

Assemble some dress-up clothes and shoes you're allowed to use; ask your guests to bring some too. Let each person dress up and wear the crown she has made. Don't forget to take pictures.

# Party Favors

Toy jewel rings, candy jewelry, chocolate coins.

# Mad Hatter's Tea Party

**J**oin Alice, the Mad Hatter, the March Hare, and the White Rabbit for a zany, topsy-turvy tea party with rabbit food, smiles without faces, wacky games, and the Queen of Heart's stolen (but now found) tarts.

# Invitations

Draw a tall hat on thin cardboard and cut it out to use as a pattern. Trace the pattern on regular or heavy-stock paper and cut it out. Decorate the front side of each hat. Fold it like an accordion, starting with the hat's brim. The hat should stand up with the brim as a base. Unfold and write the party invitation on the back; refold to mail.

# Decorations

## Outside

Read *Alice in Wonderland*, Chapter 7, to find out more about the Mad Tea Party. From posterboard or cardboard, cut out several arrows to decorate your front yard. With a dark marking pen, write TEA PARTY THIS WAY, WHITE RABBIT'S HOLE THIS WAY, MAD HATTER'S HOUSE THAT WAY, etc. on the various arrows.

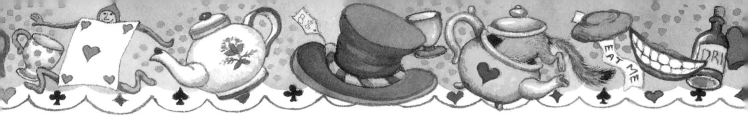

## Inside

Don't worry about elegance at this party. Use mismatched dishes and brightly colored decorations. Put out any theme-related items you might have, such as toy rabbits or mice, silly hats, or playing cards. In the middle of the table, set a small empty bottle with a tag saying DRINK ME, like the bottle Alice found and drank from just before she got very small.

## Place Cards

Get plain white paper cups and strong white paper or thin cardboard. Trace the opening of the cup on the paper and draw a wider circle around the opening for a hat brim. Cut out the bigger circle and glue it to the opening of the cup, centering the cup on the small circle. Keeping the cups upside down, write each guest's name on one with marker or pen. Decorate the hats with paint or stickers.

"Is that the reason so many tea-things are put out here?" she asked.

"Yes, that's it," said the Hatter with a sigh: "it's always tea-time, and we've no time to wash the things between whiles."

"Then you keep moving round, I suppose," said Alice.

"Exactly so," said the Hatter, "as the things get used up."

— Lewis Carroll, *Alice in Wonderland*

28

# Refreshments

- Tea Lemonade
- Cheshire Cat Smiles
- White Rabbit's Nibble Platter
- The Queen's Stolen Tarts

## Tea Lemonade

Makes 8 servings

**Ingredients:**

- 2 quarts (2 L) decaffeinated tea, cooled
- 12 ounces (360 mL) frozen lemonade concentrate
- about ¾ cup (180 mL) sugar

1. Stir tea and lemonade together until well blended.

2. Add enough sugar to sweeten to your taste. Chill.

"Take some more tea," the March Hare said to Alice, very earnestly.

"I've had nothing yet," Alice replied in an offended tone, "so I can't take more."

"You mean you can't take less," said the Hatter: "it's very easy to take more than nothing."

— Lewis Carroll, *Alice in Wonderland*

# Cheshire Cat Smiles

Makes 2 servings

**Ingredients:**

- Red apple
- 2 tablespoons (30 mL) smooth peanut butter
- 8 small marshmallows

1. With a parent's help, cut a red apple in half, remove the core, and cut it into quarter-inch-thick (6 mm) crescents.

2. Spread one side of each crescent with smooth peanut butter.

3. On one crescent, position mini marshmallows so they stick up over the edge; then top with a second slice to make a smile with teeth. Repeat with the rest of the crescents. Chill if not serving immediately.

The White Rabbit was the first resident of Wonderland that Alice met; she followed him down the rabbit hole.

## White Rabbit's Nibble Platter

Makes about 4 servings

**Ingredients:**

- 1 cup (240 mL) of uncooked vegetables: cucumbers, bell peppers, cherry tomatoes, radishes, green beans, etc.

1. Ask a parent to help you cut a variety of raw vegetables into bite-size pieces.

2. Arrange on a large platter.

The Cheshire Cat was a cat that Alice met in Wonderland. He had an amazing habit of disappearing, leaving only his smile showing.

"Herald, read the accusation!" said the King.
On this the White Rabbit blew three blasts on the trumpet, and then unrolled the parchment scroll, and read as follows:
"The Queen of Hearts, she made some tarts,
All on a summer's day:
The Knave of Hearts, he stole those tarts,
And took them quite away!"

— Lewis Carroll, *Alice in Wonderland*

# The Queen's Stolen Tarts

Makes 12 servings

**Tart Shells:**

- Cooking oil spray
- 1 tube (18 oz, 510 g) sugar cookie dough
  (or your own sugar cookie recipe)
- 6 medium-sized strawberries
- Sugar for sprinkling

**Tart Filling:**

- 8 ounces (227 g) of cream cheese, softened
- 4 tablespoons (60 mL) confectioner's sugar
- ½ cup (120 mL) heavy cream
- ½ teaspoon (2.5 mL) vanilla

1. To make the tart shells, oil a 12-cup muffin tin with cooking oil spray. Ask a parent to heat the oven to 350°F (177°C).

2. Cut a quarter-inch (6 mm) thick slice of cookie dough and push it into each muffin space so it makes a bowl with a flat bottom and has sides that go about halfway up the tin. Push the dough so that the sides are even in height and thickness. Use a fork to make marks around the rim.

3. Ask a parent to bake the tart shells for 10 to 15 minutes. They will puff up; if necessary, push the dough down slightly with your fingers when cooled to make better bowl shapes.

4. **Filling:** While the tart shells are baking, beat the filling ingredients together with an electric beater at medium speed until thick.

5. Spoon the filling into tarts when they are cooled.

6. Ask a parent to help slice strawberries in half lengthwise. Cut a small V notch in the top to make the strawberries look like hearts. Place half on each tart. Sprinkle with a little sugar.

33

# Crafts

## CRAZY HATS

You Will Need:

- 👉 **Sheets of a large newspaper**

- 👉 **Masking tape and glue**

- 👉 **Paints and paintbrushes**

- 👉 **Glitter, markers, feathers, fabric scraps**

- 👉 **Scissors and stapler**

**1.** Center four sheets of a broadsheet newspaper over your head.

**2.** Have another person wrap a band of masking tape several times around the crown of your head over the paper, just above your eye level, to shape the paper into a hat crown. Take off the hat and trim off the excess newspaper with scissors to any size brim you want.

**3.** Staple the edges together or roll up the brim and tape or staple it.

**4.** Decorate your hat with markers or paint, glitter, feathers, sequins, and fabric scraps. If you like, give awards for prettiest, silliest, biggest hat, etc.

# Games and Other Activities

## WACKY TASKS

Mark a finish line. Divide into two teams and race to the finish line. Everyone on the team must do the activity before moving on to the next. Here are some suggested challenges (some may be better suited to outside):

* Sing "Row, Row, Row Your Boat" while hanging your head upside down between your legs and walking backwards.

* With a partner, put your backs together and hook arms. Try to walk sideways while remaining attached to each other.

* Lying on your stomach and not using your arms, wiggle like a worm.

## SITTING AT THE MAD HATTER'S TABLE

In this version of musical chairs, place a plastic teacup on each chair, being sure that you have one less chair than the number of players. Play music from the movie *Alice in Wonderland* or some other music you like; when the hostess stops the music, each person tries to sit in a chair and pretends to drink tea. The person who doesn't sit in time is "out." Start the game again with one less chair. Keep going around "until things get used up," as the Hatter says.

# Party Favors

Small packs of card games (because the King and Queen in *Alice in Wonderland* were playing cards), cheap watches (like the Mad Hatter's pocket watch, which got butter in it at the tea party), kaleidoscopes, twisty straws.

# Teddy Bears' Picnic Tea Party

**T**eddy bears and other stuffed animals make perfect tea companions because they're always cheerful and hardly ever spill anything. You can plan a tea party with just your bears or invite friends to bring over their favorite stuffed animals for a picnic with lots of beary good food. If the weather isn't nice, have an indoor picnic by spreading your blanket out on the carpet.

# Invitations

Draw an outline of a teddy bear on thin cardboard and cut it out for a pattern. Trace a copy of the teddy bear onto colored paper for an invitation and cut it out. Decorate your bear with paint, glitter, stickers, ribbons, etc. Write the party information on the other side of the bear. Remind each guest to bring her favorite bear to the party.

Hostess Tip: Ask for the names of the teddy bears when you write your invitations; that way, you can put the teddy's name on the place card too.

# Decorations

## Outside

Draw and cut out several large cardboard teddy bear shapes and attach them to wood sticks to use as yard signs. Write BEAR PARTY HERE or WELCOME TEDDY FRIENDS on the bears' tummies. Attach the strings of several helium balloons to the paw of one of the bears. If the weather permits, sit a large teddy bear on your porch to "welcome" guests.

## Inside

On one bear's stomach, write WELCOME and list all the girls' and
teddies' names; then hang it in your entryway.

On accordion-folded paper, cut a chain of
bears to hang in your party room. Set extra
teddy bears around the room.

Have your table set with a red-and-white
checkered cloth. Set the cloth on the lawn if
the weather is nice. Dishes can be brightly
colored plastic or paper. Tuck several small
teddy bears into a basket for a table
centerpiece. For a small party, put out table
settings for teddy bears too.

## Place Cards

Draw a small bear on thin cardboard and cut it out for a pattern. Lay the pattern
on a piece of felt or other fabric and trace around the pattern with chalk or a
pencil. Cut out the felt bear and glue it to the front of a 2 × 3 inch (5 × 7.5 cm)
piece of paper that is folded in half. Decorate the bear with markers, or glue on
sequins and ribbons. Write the guest's name and the name of her bear on the
back. Set a felt teddy on each guest's plate.

## Refreshments

- **Hot Cocoa**
- **Beary Good Sandwiches**
- **Brown Bear Cookies**

# Hot Cocoa

Makes eight half-cup (120 mL) servings

**Ingredients:**

- ½ cup (120 mL) sugar
- ½ cup (120 mL) powdered cocoa
- 4 cups (960 mL) milk
- 1 teaspoon (5 mL) vanilla
- Cinnamon for sprinkling
- Marshmallows

1. In a medium-sized saucepan, mix sugar and cocoa, then stir in a half-cup (120 mL) of milk. Beat with a wire whisk until smooth; then stir in the rest of the milk.

2. Ask a parent to warm the mixture over medium heat until hot. Do not let it boil. Stir in vanilla. Ladle into cups. Sprinkle with cinnamon and drop a marshmallow in before serving.

## Teddy Bear Facts

The cuddly teddy bears we love today are named after the popular President of the United States, Theodore Roosevelt. In 1902, while hunting on vacation, the president refused to shoot a bear tied to a tree because it was unfair. The story made the newspapers and was fodder for a famous political cartoon. Soon after, stuffed bears were sold as "Teddy's Bears."

# Brown Bear Cookies

Makes 16 to 18 cookies

**Ingredients:**

- ¾ cup (180 mL) shortening
- 1 cup (240 mL) brown sugar, packed
- ¼ cup (60 mL) molasses
- 1 egg
- 2¼ cups (540 mL) flour
- 2 teaspoons (10 mL) baking soda
- ½ teaspoon (2.5 mL) salt
- 1 teaspoon (5 mL) ground ginger
- 1 teaspoon (5 mL) ground cinnamon
- ½ teaspoon (2.5 mL) ground cloves
- ½ cup (120 mL) granulated sugar for decoration
- Can of white icing (optional)

**1.** Have a parent preheat oven to 350°F (177°C). Cream together shortening, sugar, molasses, and egg.

**2.** Mix the dry ingredients (flour, baking soda, salt, and spices) together in a separate bowl and then stir them into the molasses mixture.

**3.** To make a bear, roll a piece of dough into a ¾-inch (2 cm) ball. This is the body. Roll a ball about half as small for the head, and make even smaller balls for the legs and arms. Spread white sugar on a plate and roll balls in it. Keep making bears with all the dough.

4. Arrange the head and body balls close together on a cookie sheet. Attach the smaller balls for the legs and arms, and finally, attach tiny balls for the ears. The dough will spread during baking and connect all the balls. Allow 2 inches (5 cm) of space around each bear.

5. Ask a parent to help you bake them, about 12 minutes. Let cool a minute, then lift off with a pancake turner, and cool on a tea towel. When cool, decorate with icing or leave plain.

# Beary Good Sandwiches

Makes two sandwiches

**Ingredients:**
- Four pieces of white bread

**Fillings (Your Choice):**
- 2 tablespoons (30 mL) of peanut butter and 2 tablespoons honey, mixed
- Cheese slices
- Sandwich meats
- Mustard

1. Make sandwiches out of white bread and cut out bear shapes with a large cookie cutter.

2. Fill one sandwich with peanut butter and honey and the other with slices of cheese and sandwich meats. Use mustard to decorate faces on cheese sandwiches if you like.

# Crafts

## DOUGH BEAR SCULPTURES

Makes enough for 4 bears

You Will Need:

 **4 cups (960 mL) flour plus extra for cutting board**

 **1 cup (240 mL) salt**

 **1½ cups (360 mL) water**

 **Plastic bag**

 **Paints or colored nail polish**

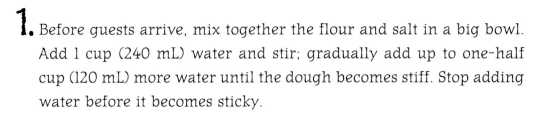

1. Before guests arrive, mix together the flour and salt in a big bowl. Add 1 cup (240 mL) water and stir; gradually add up to one-half cup (120 mL) more water until the dough becomes stiff. Stop adding water before it becomes sticky.

2. Spread a handful of flour over a cutting board or plate. Knead dough with your hands until it is soft. Wrap in a plastic bag to keep it from drying out.

3. As guests arrive, give each one a paper plate and piece of dough to work with.

4. You can make ball bears by using a big ball for the body and smaller ones for the head, legs, arms and ears. Or make flatter bear shapes and use pieces of dough to add a dress, buttons, eyes, shoes, or necklace. Use a dab of water to make the pieces stick to each other.

**5.** Don't make the bears too thick or the dough will crack when it bakes.

**6.** When everyone has finished, ask an adult to bake the bears on an ungreased cookie sheet for 45 minutes at 350°F (177°C). Allow the bears to cool for an hour; then paint them with paints or colored nail polish. Finish with a coat of clear polish for a glossy effect.

# Games and Other Activities

### BEAR DRESS-UP

Assemble a selection of doll clothes or baby clothes and hats, children's-size sunglasses, scarves, strips of lace, and costume jewelry. Let your guests dress their teddy bears.

### TEDDY BEAR MUSICAL CHAIRS

Play musical chairs carrying your teddies. To play, put out enough chairs for all guests minus one. When the music stops, instead of sitting down, put your teddy on the chair. Whoever doesn't get a chair for her teddy is out. Continue until only one player is left.

# Party Favors

Make picnic baskets out of plastic fruit baskets by weaving a quarter-inch-thick (6 mm) ribbon through the top holes. Twist the ends of a pipe cleaner through two sides of the basket to make a handle. Fill with teddy bear key chains, teddy bear stamps or stickers, pencils with bears on them, etc.

# Moms and Daughters Tea Party

To celebrate Mother's Day or another special event, invite your friends and their moms or other special adults (aunts, grandmas, etc.) to this formal party with traditional afternoon tea fare. During the height of afternoon tea's popularity in the Victorian age, wealthy English children had tea with their nannies in the nursery, not with their parents. Be glad you and your mom can enjoy this tea together.

# Invitations

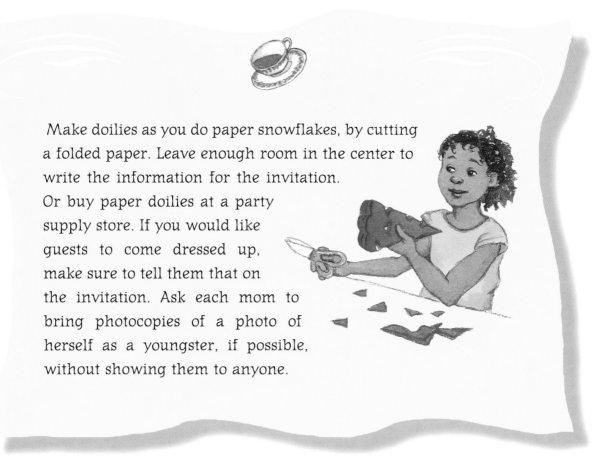

Make doilies as you do paper snowflakes, by cutting a folded paper. Leave enough room in the center to write the information for the invitation. Or buy paper doilies at a party supply store. If you would like guests to come dressed up, make sure to tell them that on the invitation. Ask each mom to bring photocopies of a photo of herself as a youngster, if possible, without showing them to anyone.

# Decorations

For this afternoon tea, use your nice tablecloth, best tea settings, and a pretty tea tray if you have it. Buy a bunch of carnations and large stickpins. Get some green flower-wrapping tape from a florist and tape the stem of one carnation for each guest. When guests arrive, give them their flowers to pin on as corsages. Since afternoon tea is not traditionally a sitting-down-at-the-table affair, place cards are not necessary.

# Refreshments

- 🍅 **Buttermilk Scones**
- 🍅 **Cambric Tea**
- 🍅 **Mock Devonshire Cream**
- 🍅 **Chocolate-Dipped Strawberries**

## Buttermilk Scones

Makes 8 scones

**Ingredients:**

- 2 cups (480 mL) flour
- 1 tablespoon (15 mL) baking powder
- 2 tablespoons (30 mL) sugar
- ½ teaspoon (2.5 mL) salt
- 4 tablespoons (60 mL) butter or margarine
- ¾ cup (180 mL) buttermilk (or milk if you don't have buttermilk)

**For Topping:**

- 1 tablespoon (15 mL) milk
- 1 tablespoon (15 mL) sugar or sugar crystals

*Note: To make cinnamon-raisin scones, add 1 teaspoon (5 mL) cinnamon and ¼ cup (60 mL) raisins to the baking mix. Instead of sprinkling just sugar on top, sprinkle a cinnamon-sugar mix.

**1.** Ask a parent to preheat the oven to 425°F (218°C).

2. Mix dry ingredients (flour, baking powder, sugar, and salt) in a large bowl.

3. Put the butter in the flour mixture and cut it up, using a pastry cutter or two butter knives, until the mixture looks like coarse bread crumbs.

4. Make a hole in the center of the dough and pour in the buttermilk. Mix with a wooden spoon just until dough forms a ball.

5. Put the dough on a floured surface and shape into a 6- to 8-inch diameter (15 to 20 cm) circle about 1½ inches (4 cm) thick. (Don't knead the scones. In fact, the less you handle the dough, the better.)

6. Brush milk on the top and sprinkle with 1 tablespoon (15 mL) sugar or decorative sugar crystals.

7. Cut the dough circle into eight wedges. Place on a baking sheet with a little space between them. Bake for about 15 minutes or until golden brown. Serve warm with jam and mock Devonshire cream.

# Cambric Tea

Makes 1 cup

**Ingredients:**

- ⅔ cup (160 mL) milk, warmed
- ⅓ cup (80 mL) decaffeinated tea
- Sugar
- ⅛ to ¼ teaspoon (about 1 mL) vanilla extract, to taste

1. Plan on at least one cup for each guest. Ask a parent to help you warm milk over low heat in a saucepan.

2. Pour milk into a cup and add tea. You can change the proportions so there is more tea, if you like. Stir in sugar and vanilla to taste.

# Mock Devonshire Cream

Makes 8 servings

**Ingredients:**

- 1 cup (240 mL) whipped topping, such as Cool Whip
- ½ cup (120 mL) sour cream
- 2 tablespoons (30 mL) confectioner's sugar

1. Place whipped topping in a bowl and fold in the sour cream and sugar.

2. Serve with jam and scones.

# Chocolate-Dipped Strawberries

Makes 12 to 15 servings

**Ingredients:**

- 25 to 35 strawberries with stems
- 6 ounces (170 g) semisweet chocolate chips

1. Wash strawberries and let them dry. Cover a baking sheet with aluminum foil. Set aside.

2. Put chocolate chips in a small microwave-safe bowl. Have a grownup heat them in the microwave on high for 1 minute and 30 seconds; stir. Heat for 45 seconds more and stir again.

3. Holding from the top, dunk strawberries halfway into the chocolate, letting the excess drip back in bowl. Lay them on the baking sheet. Reheat chocolate if it cools too much and hardens.

4. Cover strawberries and store in refrigerator.

# Games and Other Activities

## Who Is It?

Ask moms to bring photos of themselves as babies or young children without showing them to their daughters. Put all the photos in a pile. The daughters must guess which picture belongs to which mom.

## Mom—Daughter Guessing Game

Form teams of two people, each with a mom and her daughter. Ask a personal question and have each mom write down what she thinks her daughter would answer; have the daughter write what she thinks the mom would answer. Each correct answer gains a point for the mom-daughter team that guessed correctly.

Some possible questions: "What is your favorite (food, color, candy bar, pop)?" "If you have free time, what do you do?"

# Crafts

## Scrapbook Page

You Will Need:

- 👉 **Looseleaf-sized paper**
- 👉 **Photocopy of each mom's picture**
- 👉 **Markers, stickers, etc. for decorating**
- 👉 **Pencils and glue**

**1.** After you have played the "Who Is It?" game, invite each girl to interview her mom and ask where she lived, how many brothers and sisters she had, and what her favorite games, food, music, toys, etc. were when she was young.

2. Each girl should paste a photocopy of a picture of her mom on a looseleaf-sized piece of paper and write down some of the things she discovered. She can then decorate the page with markers and stickers.

3. After everyone is done, have someone read the pages to all the guests. Each girl's page can become the start of a scrapbook project.

# Party Favors

In a party bag for each guest, put a scented soap and potpourri sachet.

# Garden Tea Party

**T**he garden is a lovely spot for a spring or summer tea party. The sunshine and fresh air will encourage appetites. A yard gives you room for outside games with a large group; a shady tree can offer a sheltered spot for an intimate picnic with a couple of friends. Make spring bonnets and end with a grand garden parade.

# Invitations

Draw a butterfly on thin cardboard and cut it out to serve as a pattern. For each guest, trace around the butterfly pattern on construction paper. Cut out the butterflies and decorate them with markers, paper, and glue. Write the party information on back.

# Decorations

If possible, set a table outside on the lawn or under a shady tree. Use real flowers as a centerpiece or make tissue paper flowers with pipe cleaner stems; put in vases. Keep the table settings simple with flower-patterned paper plates, but use real teacups if possible. If you only have a couple of guests, you could lay out a blanket under a low tree or tall bush and have a secret party, partly hidden under the branches. Make butterflies (see Crafts section) and hang them around the house or garden.

# Place Cards

Collect a few pretty rocks and use pens or paint to write each girl's name on a rock. Use the rocks to hold down napkins on the table so the wind doesn't blow them away.

# Refreshments

- 🦋 **Homemade Lemonade**
- 🦋 **Blossom Ice Cubes**
- 🦋 **Herb Flower Sandwiches**
- 🦋 **Peanut ButterFlies**

## Homemade Lemonade

Makes 18 half-cup servings of lemonade

**Ingredients:**
- 9 lemons
- 1¼ cups (300 mL) sugar (or more, to taste)
- 7 cups (1680 mL) water

1. Juice 8 lemons. You should get about two cups (480 mL) of juice.

2. Mix sugar, lemon juice, and water in a large pitcher. Ask a parent to help you slice the remaining lemon into slices.

3. Float slices in pitcher. Serve over blossom ice cubes.

# Blossom Ice Cubes

**Ingredients:**

- Edible flower blossoms
- Boiled water

1. Pick edible flower blossoms from pesticide-free plants. Edible flowers include roses, pansies, violets, nasturtiums, and lavender. Ask if not sure. Many flowers are poisonous.

2. Place blossoms in the bottom of an empty ice tray. Fill each compartment with a little water or lemonade and freeze. Take ice tray out of the freezer and fill with water or lemonade to the top and freeze again. If you are serving lemonade punch-style and want an ice ring for the lemonade bowl, follow the same procedure, but use a ring mold or a bundt cake pan instead of individual cubes.

# Herb Flower Sandwiches

Makes 8 sandwiches

**Ingredients:**

- 4 to 6 tablespoons (60 to 90 mL) of chopped fresh herbs such as chives, parsley, or thyme
- 8 tablespoons (120 mL) of softened cream cheese
- 16 slices of white bread
- Carrot and small celery stalks

1. Mix the chopped fresh herbs through the softened cream cheese with a fork.

2. Spread a tablespoon (15 mL) of cheese on eight slices of bread, and top each with a plain slice of bread. Use a scalloped biscuit cutter or round glass to cut the sandwiches into flower shapes or circles.

3. Ask a parent to cut the carrot into circular slices.

4. Place the flower sandwich on a plate. Dab a bit of cream cheese on the back of a round carrot slice and place it in the middle of the flower. Stick a small celery stalk with leaves on the plate below the flower for a stem.

# Peanut ButterFlies

See dough package for servings

**Ingredients:**

- One tube of refrigerator peanut butter cookie dough*
- Heart-shaped pretzel twists and thin pretzel sticks
- Cooking oil spray

*Or use your own favorite peanut butter cookie recipe.

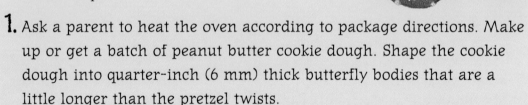

1. Ask a parent to heat the oven according to package directions. Make up or get a batch of peanut butter cookie dough. Shape the cookie dough into quarter-inch (6 mm) thick butterfly bodies that are a little longer than the pretzel twists.

2. Place two pretzel twists next to each other on an oiled cookie sheet with the bottoms of the hearts touching. Put one of the butterfly bodies in the middle and press it into the pretzels.

3. Break a pretzel stick in half and push the halves into the top of the body to make antennae.

4. Ask a parent to help you bake them until golden brown, about 11 to 13 minutes, and to help you remove them from the oven. Let cool for a minute, then move with a pancake turner to a wire rack to cool.

57

# Crafts

## GARDEN BONNETS

You Will Need:

 **Inexpensive straw hats\***

 **Things to decorate them: paint, pens, glitter, etc.**

 **Strong glue and stapler**

 **Crepe paper streamers**

**\*If you don't buy straw hats, get large white paper plates and large paper bowls, 1 plate and 1 bowl for each partygoer, plus some extras.**

Decorate inexpensive straw hats from a craft store or make your own paper bonnets. Then have a hat parade around the garden.

To make a paper bonnet:

**1.** Center a plain white paper bowl on a large white paper plate. Trace a circle around the bowl on the plate. Draw another circle a half-inch (1 cm) smaller than the bowl inside the big circle you drew, and cut out this smaller circle so there is a hole in the middle of the plate and you are left with a paper ring.

**2.** Turn the bowl and plate upside down. Glue the rim of the bowl on top of the paper ring to form a wide-brimmed hat. Make hats for each of your guests.

**3.** Let each girl decorate her own hat. Staple crepe paper streamers at the sides for ties.

## BUTTERFLIES

You Will Need:

- 👉 **White coffee filters**

- 👉 **Watercolor paints**

- 👉 **Paintbrushes**

- 👉 **Plates you can work on**

- 👉 **Wooden clothespins**

- 👉 **Construction paper**

**1.** Dab watercolor paints on white coffee filters. Keep the painted filter on a plate, as the colors will soak through. (If you place the filter on newspaper, the black ink might run.)

**2.** When the paint dries, fold the filter like an accordion with small folds. Pinch in the middle and clip the middle with a wooden clothespin, which will be the body of the butterfly. Fan out the butterfly's wings.

**3.** Cut thin strips of construction paper for antennae and glue to body.

# Games and Other Activities

### DRINK UP THE TEA

Place a teacup on a chair at one end of the lawn and a bowl of water and teaspoons at the other end. Girls split into teams and do a relay to see which group can fill the teacup first by walking with teaspoons of water.

### GARDEN SCAVENGER HUNT

1. Before the party, write out a list of things you can find in a garden (for example, a rock, a leaf, a weed). Make at least a couple of the items hard to find.

2. Decide if you want guests to collect items as they find them (make sure it's OK with your parents) or to write down where they are located. Divide the guests up into several groups. If girls are going to pick up scavenger items, give them bags; make sure they have pencils and paper if they are writing instead. If you like, have a prize for the group that finds all the things first.

# Party Favors

Flowerpot with seedlings (see below); seed packets, butterfly or insect stickers, or a small set of garden tools tucked into a pair of child-size gardening gloves.

### FLOWERPOTS WITH SEEDLINGS

Get small, inexpensive terra cotta pots. Decorate the outsides of the pots with acrylic paints, if you wish. Get potting soil and spring or summer flower seedlings that are ready to transplant. Plant one or two seedlings in each pot for the girls to take home as party favors.

## Some Tea History

* There are more than 2000 varieties of *Camellia sinensis*, the evergreen shrub that supplies tea leaves. It is a relative of the shiny-leafed camellia shrub grown in gardens.

* Tea began gaining popularity in England in the 1660s, though at first only the very rich could afford it. By the early 1700s tea sales were booming and overtook coffee in popularity in England.

# Literary Tea Party

A cup of tea is a relaxing drink to sip while reading a favorite book, so what better than a tea party celebrating books? You can focus your tea on a specific book or make it more general. Some good books that mention drinking tea include LITTLE WOMEN, ANNE OF GREEN GABLES, AND THE SECRET GARDEN. This party could also be adapted for a mother-daughter book club event.

# Invitations

For each invitation, fold a piece of letter-sized paper in quarters to make a little "book." Decorate the front of each like a book jacket. Make up a title for your book, such as THE BEST TEA PARTY by [Your Name]. Write all the party information inside. Draw pictures on any blank pages. Ask each guest to bring one of her favorite books to share. If you like, invite each guest to come dressed as her favorite children's book character.

"You can ask Diana to come over and spend the afternoon with you and have tea here."
"Oh, Marilla!" Anne clasped her hands. "How perfectly lovely. You are able to imagine things after all or else you'd never have understood how I've longed for that very thing. It will seem so nice and grown-uppish. No fear of my forgetting to put the tea to draw when I have company."

— Lucy Maud Montgomery, *Anne of Green Gables*

# Decorations

Get posters about reading from the library. Write quotes from well-known books on helium balloons with a permanent-ink pen. Place children's books around the room and use a stack of books as a table centerpiece.

# Place Cards

For each one cut a rectangle of thick paper that is 2 × 3 inches (5 × 7.5 cm). Fold in half. Write a guest's name on the outside of each one. Decorate with drawings of books or favorite story characters.

# Refreshments

- **Orange Tea Punch**
- **Anne's Ginger Snaps**
- **Garden Banana Muffins**

"I am better. She makes me better. The nurse must bring up her tea with mine. We will have tea together. . ."

"They are always wanting me to eat things when I don't want to," said Colin, as the nurse brought in the tea and put it on the table by the sofa. "Now, if you'll eat, I will. Those muffins look so nice and hot."

— Frances Hodgson Burnett, *The Secret Garden*

# Orange Tea Punch

Makes 10 to 12 servings

**Ingredients:**

- 12 oz (360 mL) frozen orange juice concentrate
- 2 cups (480 mL) brewed decaffeinated orange spice tea, cooled
- 2 cups (480 mL) cranberry juice cocktail

Mix ingredients in a pitcher or punch bowl and chill until ready to serve.

"Oh, Marilla, can I use the rosebud spray tea set?"
"No, indeed! The rosebud tea set! Well, what next? You know I never use that except for the minister or the Aids [Ladies Aid Society]. You'll put down the old brown tea set. . . And you can cut some fruit-cake and have some of the cookies and snaps."
"I can just imagine myself sitting down at the head of the table and pouring the tea," said Anne, shutting her eyes ecstatically. "And asking Diana if she takes sugar! I know she doesn't but of course I'll ask her just as if I didn't know."

— Lucy Maud Montgomery, *Anne of Green Gables*

# Anne's Ginger Snaps

Makes about 45 cookies

**Ingredients:**

- ¾ cup (180 mL) shortening
- 1 cup (240 mL) brown sugar, packed
- ¼ cup (60 mL) molasses
- 1 egg
- 2¼ cups (540 mL) cups flour
- 2 teaspoons (10 mL) baking soda
- ½ teaspoon (2.5 mL) salt
- 1 teaspoon (5 mL) ground ginger
- 1 teaspoon (5 mL) ground cinnamon
- ½ teaspoon (2.5 mL) ground cloves
- Granulated sugar

1. Ask a parent to heat oven to 350°F (177°C). With a mixer, cream together shortening, brown sugar, molasses, and egg.

2. Mix the flour, baking soda, salt, ginger, cinnamon, and cloves together in a separate bowl and then stir into the molasses mixture.

3. Roll dough into 1-inch (2.5 cm) balls. Spread granulated sugar on a plate and roll the balls in it.

4. Arrange them on a cookie sheet and leave 2 inches (5 cm) around each ball. Ask a parent to help you bake them, for about 12 minutes. Let cool a minute; lift off with a pancake turner and cool on a tea towel.

# Garden Banana Muffins

Makes about 18 muffins

**Ingredients:**

- Cooking oil spray
- 1 cup (240 mL) sugar
- 1 cup (240 mL) (two medium) mashed bananas
- ¼ cup (60 mL) applesauce
- ¼ cup (60 mL) butter or margarine, softened
- ¼ cup (60 mL) milk
- 1 teaspoon (5 mL) vanilla
- 2 eggs
- 2 cups (480 mL) flour
- 1 teaspoon (5 mL) baking soda
- ½ teaspoon (2.5 mL) salt
- ½ cup (120 mL) chopped nuts or chocolate chips (optional)

1. Ask a parent to heat oven to 350°F (177°C). Oil a muffin tin.

2. In a large bowl, blend sugar, bananas, applesauce, butter, milk, eggs, and vanilla.

3. In a separate bowl, mix the dry ingredients (flour, baking soda, and salt). Stir the dry ingredients into the wet batter only until all is moistened. Add nuts or chocolate chips if you wish to.

4. Pour into the oiled muffin pan. Ask a parent to bake until done, about 20 to 25 minutes. Cool 5 minutes; then remove from pan and cool completely.

# Crafts

## BOOKMARKS AND BOOKPLATES

You Will Need:

**Ribbon**

**Markers, stickers, stamps, etc.**

**Plain white self-stick postal labels**

**Posterboard**

**Bookmarks:** Make bookmarks out of strips of posterboard or wide ribbons. Decorate with markers, stickers, or stamps.

**Bookplates:** Write "This book belongs to . . ." on large self-stick postal labels, and let each guest decorate some. Add to party favors.

# Games and Other Activities

## LITERARY SKIT

In advance of the party, pick a scene from a familiar book to perform as a skit. Make sure there are enough characters for all the guests at the party. Provide dress-up clothes for each character if possible. Discuss the basic plot of the skit

and let each girl improvise her part. Keep the dialogue simple. When you are ready, do a rehearsal in costumes. Put on a performance for the parents when they come to pick up the guests, or videotape it for posterity.

### STORY TIME

Have each guest bring a favorite book and ask her to read a short passage.

# Party Favors

Give each guest a small blank book. Decorate the covers with stickers or pictures if you wish. Put a notebook and a pretty pencil in a party bag for each guest.

# Pajama Tea Party

**T**his tea could work as the end of a slumber party or as a morning brunch party. Ask everyone to wear pajamas and slippers. After enjoying yummy breakfast foods, such as cinnamon-raisin bread and fruit, guests can decorate pillows, play games, and get pedicures.

# Invitations

Draw a muffin outline on thin cardboard and cut it out to use as a pattern. Trace the muffin shape on a card-sized piece of construction paper or on the front of a piece of plain card stock. Decorate the front and write your party invitation on the inside.

# Decorations

Decorate your party room to look like an old-time diner with a checkered tablecloth, white placemats, and salt and pepper shakers. Use a piece of posterboard to make a large menu display, and list prices on it. Don't forget to include Today's Special! You could also make individual menus and write down what you are serving for breakfast on them.

# Refreshments

- 🍅 **Chocolate Mint Tea**
- 🍅 **Pinwheels**
- 🍅 **Cinnamon-Raisin Bread**
- 🍅 **Fruit Platter with Dip**

## Chocolate Mint Tea

Makes 4 half-cup (120 mL) servings

**Ingredients:**
- 1 peppermint tea bag
- 2 cups (480 mL) of boiling water
- 6 tablespoons (90 mL) instant hot cocoa mix

1. Have a parent help you boil and pour water over a peppermint tea bag. Steep for at least 5 minutes.

2. Add hot cocoa mix to tea and stir well. Serve hot.

# Pinwheels

Makes 1 serving

**Ingredients:**

- 2 slices thinly sliced white bread

**Topping (Your Choice):**

- 1 tablespoon (15 mL) peanut butter, jelly, or cream cheese
- 2 slices thinly sliced cooked meats
- 1 teaspoon (5 mL) mayonnaise if you use meat

1. Spread or place your chosen topping on a piece of thin-sliced white bread. Ask a parent to help you trim off the crusts.

2. Using two hands, roll up the slice with the topping inside. If necessary, hold it shut with toothpicks.

3. Wrap the roll in waxed paper and twist the paper ends or tape them shut.

4. Chill in refrigerator for two hours. Before serving, unwrap the rolls and ask a parent to help you cut quarter-inch-thick (6 mm) slices across the rolls. Remove toothpicks if you used them. Lay pinwheels on their sides to serve.

Make as many sandwiches as you need, using different toppings.

# Cinnamon-Raisin Bread

Makes 8 servings

- ¼ cup (60 mL) butter or margarine, softened
- ½ cup (120 mL) brown sugar, packed
- 2 eggs
- ¼ cup (60 mL) applesauce
- ½ cup (120 mL) honey
- ½ cup (120 mL) milk
- 2 cups (480 mL) flour
- 1 teaspoon (5 mL) baking soda
- 1 teaspoon (5 mL) baking powder
- 1 tablespoon (15 mL) cinnamon
- ¼ teaspoon (1 mL) salt
- 1 cup (240 mL) raisins
- Cooking oil spray

1. Ask a parent to heat oven to 325°F (163°C).

2. Cream butter and sugar until smooth. Add eggs one at a time and beat the mixture until fluffy.

3. Blend honey, applesauce, and buttermilk into the mixture.

4. In a separate bowl, mix the dry ingredients together (flour, baking soda, baking powder, cinnamon, and salt). Then blend the dry ingredients into the creamed mixture. Stir in raisins.

5. Pour the mixture into an oiled loaf pan. Ask a parent to bake it for 1 hour, or until done.

6. Remove from oven and cool in pan for 10 minutes; then turn the bread out onto a rack to cool completely.

# Fruit Platter with Dip

Allow the equivalent of about one apple's worth of fruit per person

**Ingredients:**

- Variety of seasonal fruit

**For Dip:**

- 1 cup (240 mL) whipped topping, such as Cool Whip
- 1 cup (240 mL) fruit-flavored yogurt

1. Ask a parent to help cut a variety of fresh seasonal fruit such as watermelon, cantaloupe, apples, oranges, and strawberries, into bite-sized pieces.

2. With slippery or juicy fruit, poke toothpicks into the fruit chunks to make them easier to pick up. Arrange on a platter around a bowl of dip.

3. To make the dip, blend whipped topping with fruit yogurt. Cover and chill everything if not serving immediately.

# Crafts

## SWEET DREAMS PILLOWCASES

You Will Need:

**Plain pillowcases, one for each girl**

**Cardboards**

**Permanent markers or fabric paint***

***Note: Don't use the puffy kind of paint — it won't be comfortable against your face.**

**1.** Buy inexpensive, solid-colored pillowcases. Put a piece of cardboard inside each pillowcase and let the girls draw pictures on the pillowcases with permanent markers or fabric paint.

**2.** Let the pictures dry; then remove the cardboard.

# Games and Other Activities

### Beauty Salon

Pair off and have guests give pedicures to each other. You can do a full treatment by soaking feet and then rubbing them with lotion, or just paint toenails with a bright polish. Chill used tea bags and give two to each girl to put over her eyes as she relaxes during her pedicure.

### Pass the Envelope

Fill an envelope with silly instructions, such as "Sing a song with a marshmallow in your mouth," "Draw a picture blindfolded," "Make a silly face," "Tell a joke," and "Say a tongue twister three times." Pass the envelope around with music on. The hostess turns off the music after a minute or two. The person left holding the envelope when the music stops has to pull out a slip of paper and do whatever instruction is on it.

Hostess tip: Make sure to have any necessary materials mentioned in the silly instructions on hand.

# Party Favors

Give each guest some scented drawer sachets and a bottle of clear nail polish to take home in her decorated pillowcase.

# Index